When there is separation, there is coming together.
When there is coming together, there is dissolution.
All things may become one, whatever their state of being.
Only he who has transcended sees this oneness.

Chuang Tzu
(third century B.C.)

Bamboo

Thirty spokes share one hub. Make the nothing therein appropriate, and you will have the use of the cart.

Knead clay in order to make a vessel. Make the nothing therein appropriate, and you will have the use of the clay vessel.

Cut out doors and windows in order to make a room. Make the nothing therein appropriate, and you will have the use of the room.

Thus we gain by making it Something, but we have the use by making it Nothing.

Lao Tzu, *Tao Te Ching*
(sixth century B.C.)

The Emperor Wu Ti

To know yet to think that one does not know

      is the best;

Not to know yet to think that one knows

      will put one in difficulty.

That the sage meets with no difficulty

      is because he is alive to difficulty.

That is why he meets with no difficulty.

Lao Tzu, Tao Te Ching

The whole world says that I am vast, vast and resemble nothing. It is because I resemble nothing that I am able to be vast. If I resembled anything, I would, long before now, have become small.

Now I constantly have three treasures
Which I hold and cherish.
The first is known as compassion,
The second is known as frugality,
The third is known as not daring to take the lead
        in the empire;
Compassionate, I am able to be courageous;
Frugal, I am able to be extensive;
Not daring to take the lead in the empire,
        I am able to be lord over the complete vessels.

Now to forsake my compassion for courage, my frugality for expansion, to give up my position in the rear for the lead, is sure to end in death.

Through compassion, I can triumph in war and be impregnable in defense.

When heaven sets up something, it keeps it, as it were, behind ramparts of compassion.

Lao Tzu, *Tao Te Ching*

Before the Cascade

Governing a large state is like boiling a small fish.

When the empire is ruled in accordance with the way, the spirits are not potent. Or, rather, it is not that they are not potent, but that in their potency they do not harm men. It is not only they who, in their potency, do not harm men, the sage, too, does not harm them. Now as neither does any harm, each attributes the merit to the other.

Lao Tzu, *Tao Te Ching*

Lao Tzu Seated on His Buffalo

He who knows others is clever;
He who knows himself has discernment.
He who overcomes others has force;
He who overcomes himself has strength.

Mount Hua

He who knows contentment is rich;
He who perseveres in action has purpose.
Not to lose one's station is to endure;
Not to be forgotten when dead is to be long lived.

Lao Tzu, *Tao Te Ching*

I attain the utmost emptiness;
I keep to extreme stillness.
The myriad creatures all rise together
And I watch thereby their return.
The teeming creatures
All return to their separate roots.
Returning to one's roots is known as stillness.
Stillness is what is called returning to one's destiny.
Returning to one's destiny is normal.
Knowledge of the normal is discernment.
Not to know the normal is to be without basis.
To innovate without basis bodes ill.
To know the normal is to be tolerant.
Tolerance leads to impartiality,
Impartiality to kingliness,
Kingliness to heaven,
Heaven to the way,
The way to perpetuity,
And to the end of one's days
      one will meet with no danger.

Lao Tzu, *Tao Te Ching*

Peasants Welcoming the Dragon

Life and death, profit and loss, failure and success, poverty and wealth, value and worthlessness, praise and blame, hunger and thirst, cold and heat— these are natural changes in the order of things. They alternate with one another like day and night. No one knows where one ends and the other begins. Therefore, they should not disturb our peace or enter into our souls. Live so that you are at ease, in harmony with the world, and full of joy. Day and night, share the springtime with all things, thus creating the seasons in your own heart. This is called achieving full harmony.

Chuang Tzu

Once I, Chuang Tzu, dreamed that I was a butterfly and was happy as a butterfly. I was conscious that I was quite pleased with myself, but I did not know that I was Tzu. Suddenly I awoke, and there I was, visibly Tzu. I do not know whether it was Tzu dreaming that he was a butterfly or the butterfly dreaming that it was Tzu. Between Tzu and the butterfly there must be some distinction. This is called the transformation of things.

Chuang Tzu

The Scholar's Nap

Beneath the rain

See the sun shining

In its flames

Drink at the cool source.

Anonymous

雨中看果日
火裏酌清泉

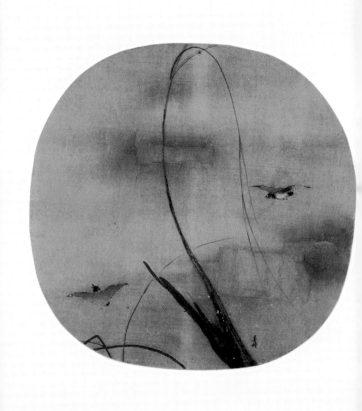

Thus knowledge is the preservation of life. Fail not to observe the four seasons and to adapt to cold and heat, to bring into harmony joy and anger and to be calm both in repose and in one's actions, to reconcile the Yin and Yang and to balance the hard and the soft.

In this way, having warded off the coming of the wicked, life shall be long and vision lasting.

The Ling Shu
A Chinese medical treatise of the Sung dynasty

Birds with a Weeping Willow Branch

Confucius was traveling in the Kingdom of Ch'u. In a clearing he saw a hunchback who was bringing down flying grasshoppers as easily as if he had picked them up. "You are very skilled," he said to him. "Tell me your secret."

"It is this," said the hunchback. "I practiced for five or six months by holding balls balanced on my cane. When I could hold two, I only missed a few grasshoppers. When I could hold three, I only missed one in ten. When I was able to hold five, I took grasshoppers in flight with my cane as surely as I could pick things by hand. Neither my body nor my arm has nervous tremors any more. My concentration is never distracted by anything. In this immense universe filled with so many beings, I see only the grasshopper at which I aim, so I never miss it."

Confucius looked at his disciples and said to them, "Concentration of his will on a single object has produced perfect cooperation between his mind and body."

Taking his turn to speak, the hunchback said to Confucius, "But you are a scholar, why have you been questioning me? Why do you wish to know about something that is none of your business? Sweep away those principles of yours before you talk about it again."

Lieh Tzu
The True Classic of Complete Emptiness (fifth century B.C.)

The Poet Lin Pu Wandering in Moonlight

That which transforms things and fits them together is called change; that which stimulates
them and sets them in motion is called continuity.
That which raises them up and sets them forth before
all people on earth is called the field of action.

The I Ching
Ta Chuan (The Great Commentary), part 1

In war the victorious strategist only seeks battle after the victory has been won, whereas he who is destined to defeat first fights and afterwards looks for victory.

Sun Tzu
The Art of War
(third century B.C.)

Horsemen in the Spring

The superior man will give only names

that can be described in speech

and say only what can be carried out in practice.

Horseman and His Mount

With regard to his speech,

the superior man does not take it lightly.

Confucius
The Analects, 13:3
(fourth century B.C.)

You call the Six Classics the great sun and lack of learning the long night. But if you saw the lecture hall as nothing but a grave hut, and took all that chanting and reciting to be the words of ghosts; if you saw the Six Classics as nothing but overgrown weeds, and benevolence and righteousness as the stinking, rotting flesh; if you realized that all this staring at documents and records makes your eyes go weak, and all this bowing and saluting makes you hunched over and crooked; that wearing the insignia robes twists your muscles, and discussing the rites and canons makes your teeth rot—then you would reject the whole lot and begin anew with the ten thousand things.

Hsi Kang (223–262)
"A Refutation of Chang Miao's Essay
'People Naturally Delight in Learning'"

Shih Te Laughing beneath the Moon

Today I sat before the cliff...

A thousand yards the green peaks lift their heads.

White clouds, and the morning light is still;

Moonrise, and the lamp of night drifts upward—

Body free from dust and strain,

What cares could trouble my mind?

Han Shan
(late sixth century A.D.)

Landscape

To judge a thing is to bring to light what one sees.

To speak is to give voice to what is in one's heart.

If one is truly capable, one appears so.

There is a proverb that says,

"What's the use of splitting hairs,

  it is better to listen."

Wang Fu (90–165)

An Evening Gathering at the Scholar Han Hsi Tzai's

The lute and poetry can give us delight;

Long rambles are a joy.

I keep the Tao in me and evolve alone,

Rejecting all knowledge, abandoning my body,

Solitary and unencumbered,

What would I seek in others?

Haunting magic peaks

I'll quiet my desires and nurture my mind.

Hsi Kang

Li Po Declaiming a Poem

An Autumn Evening in the Mountains

After rain the empty mountain
Stands autumnal in the evening,
Moonlight in its groves of pine,
Stones of crystal in its brooks.
Bamboos whisper of washer-girls bound home,
Lotus-leaves yield before a fisher-boat —
And what does it matter that springtime has gone,
While you are here, O Prince of Friends?

Wang Wei (701–761)

Before the Mountain

At the Cell of an Absent Mountain Priest

By a stony wall I enter the Red Valley.
The pine tree gate is choked up with green moss;
There are bird marks on the deserted steps,
But none to open the door of the priest's cell.
I peer through the window and see his white brush*
Hung on the wall and covered with dust.
Disappointed, I sigh in vain;
I would go, but loiter wistfully about.
Sweet scented clouds are wafted along the mountainside,
And a rain of flowers falls from the sky.
Here I may taste the bliss of solitude
And listen to the plaint of blue monkeys.
Ah, what tranquillity reigns over this ground!
What isolation from all things of the world!

Li Po (700?–762)

*A priest's white brush is carried as a symbol of purity and cleanliness.

Monkeys in a Tree

Selected Bibliography

In English, the *Tao Te Ching* remains one of the most frequently translated piece of writing from the Chinese. Scholarship (and translation) of the *Tao Te Ching* has moreover benefited greatly in recent years from the unearthing of silk manuscripts of the text at Ma Wang Tui in 1973, providing a version that is earlier and far more elaborate than what was previously available. The new D. C. Lau translation for Everyman's Library (Knopf, 1994; also available from Penguin) quoted in this volume, is based on the Ma Wang Tui manuscripts. The Lau translation also exists in a scholarly edition: *Chinese Classics: Tao Te Ching* (Hong Kong: Chinese University Press, 1982), which includes translations of both the Wang Pi and the Ma Wang Tui editions, together with the original Chinese texts. See also:

Chen, Ellen M. *Tao Te Ching: A New Translation and Commentary*. New York: Paragon House, 1989.

English, Jane, and Gia-Fu Feng. *Tao Te Ching*. New York: Knopf, 1974.

Henricks, Robert G. *Lao-tzu Te-tao Ching: A New Translation Based on the Recently Discovered Ma-wang-tui Texts*. London: The Bodley Head, 1990.

Lin, Paul J. *A Translation of Lao Tzu's Tao Te Ching and Wang Pi's Commentary*. Ann Arbor: University of Michigan Press, 1977.

ther Taoist Texts and Collections of Related Poetry:

Bynner, Witter. *The Chinese Translations*. New York: Farrar, Straus & Giroux, 1978.

Chan, Wing-Tsit. *A Source Book in Chinese Philosophy*. Princeton: Princeton University Press, 1963 (reprint 1973).

English, Jane, and Gia-Fu Feng. *Chuang Tsu*. New York: Knopf, 1974.

Giles, Lionel. *Sun Tzŭ, The Art of War*. London: Hodder & Stoughton, 1981.

Graham, A. C. *Chuang Tzu: The Inner Chapters*. London: George Allen & Unwin, 1981.

Graham, A. C. *The Book of Lieh-tzŭ*. New York: Columbia University Press, 1990.

Henricks, Robert G. *Philosophy and Argumentation in Third-Century China: The Essays of Hsi K'ang*. Princeton: Princeton University Press, 1983.

Legge, James. *I Ching*. New York: Dover, 1963.

Seth, Vikram. *Three Chinese Poets*. Boston: Faber and Faber, 1992.

Watson, Burton. *Cold Mountain: One Hundred Poems by Han-shan*. London: Jonathan Cape, 1970.

Wu, John C. H. *Chinese Literature: A Historical Introduction*. New York: Ronald Press Co., 1961.